Amazing and Exciting
Truths and Laws
About Human Beings
AND OF
God

KRISTEN MARIE PLAYER

Paperback: 978-1-969919-09-1
eBook: 978-1-969919-10-7
Library of Congress Control Number: 2025921390

This is a work of nonfiction.

Ordering Information:

Prime Seven Media
518 Landmann St.
Tomah City, WI 54660

Printed in the United States of America

lways believe in The Lord Jesus Christ Almighty. You will always be with God forever on Earth and in The Kingdom of Heaven For All of Eternity. God will decide when it is your time to be with God in The Paradise of Heaven For All of Eternity. Don't ever fear death as after you die you will be born into Eternal Life with your Father God Almighty Forever and Ever. Always believe in The Lord your God. God has given you life and every person who is in your life. God is love.

When you like yourself as you are you will see the bad habits you used to have will disappear. Make your own space in your own home. Your own space of rest gathering of your thoughts. With your good experiences you have had and that are to come. And a place of your own where you can organize yourself for greater opportunities. That you can make for yourself to become a part of your world. Everything that has happened to you in your life has meant to of happened for you. To be where you are at in your life now and these experiences have made you the person you are.

God created you by giving you life on this Earth. God has been with you through everything you have experienced in your entire life time past present future. God's love is everlasting on Earth and in the Kingdom of Heaven. God will continue to bless you with God's loving kindness countless blessings. As you like the rest of us are very precious and valuable to God. God will always love you as God's love is eternal and everlasting. God will always bless you with lots of wonderful surprises each and every day you live. When you do good in your life you will see how good things that are Happening to you and Coming your way. We are all examples Of each other with how we live our lives by everything we do and by how we are as individuals. We are all learning from our own experiences and from every person we know from people we come across during our days and from people we are yet to meet in the future by being at places like at the right time and place. We are forever growing changing learning from our experiences giving out words of comfort joy and wisdom. By giving out these warm gestures of.

Ourselves to people we are receiving all these things in return. When you respect yourself and like yourself as you are you are able to bring out the best in people you know. You can learn to look on the positive side of everything you go through. This will help you to work out your deepest concerns. When you realize when you see the positive side of these hurdles that these things you thought were becoming an issue for you weren't as. Concerning for you because you handled yourself with these issues in a positive way.

The way to win friends is to always be respectful considerate kind hearted good willed fair just genuine sincere honest trustworthy. People will treat you the way you treat them. As this is how we all learn from each other. You will gain more fulfillment when you are patient thoughtful understanding supportive to people you know and to people you come across. What you reap is what you will sow. Always be there for those special people you care for the most. By continuing to be respectful considerate kind hearted good willed Supportive fair just genuine sincere honest trustworthy. To Them this is what makes true good Solid genuine friendships. That will last for a lifetime. Every day we are experiencing God's presence. We will continue to experience God's presence every day for the rest of our days on this Earth until the last day. When we die our souls will be taken to The Almighty. Fear nothing as God is always with you guiding you and protecting you at every moment you live. We are all in God's capable hands Forever and ever. On Earth and in The Paradise of Heaven. Thank God for every waking and sleeping moment. That God is giving you to live.

Always love everyone you come across every day you live your life. We are in Gods capable hands always and we always will be forever. After we serve our purpose on this Earth we will have Eternal life in the Kingdom of Heaven where we will experience complete joy of love from Our Father. There will be no more suffering of worries fears and insecurities. We will be with complete bliss harmony peace and love. God loves you as God is your provider. Give your praises of thanks to God as God has given you life on this.

Earth. God has a place for you to have Eternal life in the Kingdom of Heaven when God decides you have served your purposes on this Earth. Fear nothing as God is with you always. No matter what happens to you in your life God is with you all the way through your entire stay on this Earth. God has a plan for you He will reveal this plan to you in good time. God will continue to bless you every day of your life. Honour your Father the Almighty as God is guiding you in your life. God has put those special people in your life for you To rejoice to learn to gain support from and visa versa to Share both of your experiences with to relate to one another. Know that these people will always be there for you because they are so interested in your wellbeing. These people want to be there for you that's why they are. You have a purpose and reasons why you are here on this Earth. You will discover these reasons by living your life. Be open with yourself and other people to work it all out. As life is short why not do what you have always dreamed of doing. Make your dreams come true by making these things become a part of your.

World. You have all the answers to everything you go through. For you to discover these answers you need to have good solid friendships with some people you connect very well with completely. These people are helping you to become the person you are. That you are that they are helping you to gain strength within yourself. For you to take on even greater opportunities in your life. In the right time.

When these opportunities are meant to come your way. Learn from everything you go through. Know you don't have to be a friend to anyone you don't want to be friends with. Learn to say no to people at times as this can prevent you from being walked over. At times in your life you will need to stand your ground with people you come across at work operators with your neighbours and with your family. Look out for your true friends by offering your honest support to them. As these people are the people who you treasure cherish validate help support welcome the most in your life. Know that these people will always be there for you just like.

You will always be there for them. We all want to feel wanted respected cared for understood accepted important and worthy of our efforts with what we put into our friendships. At work where you study at church of your interests at home and with your partner. There are reasons for everything you go through for you to learn to gain insight of knowledge. To help you to understand yourself and other people better. To gain wisdom and for you to gain more confidence within.

Yourself. As you are to take on greater and more adventures goals in your life. Always be open to new ideas as one thing leads to another. This way you will have choices with what you are interested in doing. You are then in a much better position to make the decision of what suits you the most. Break free from the people that cause you pain the most. You have your life to live. Turn to those people in your life you feel who understand you and who you feel you connect well with. You don't have to see those people you feel are causing you complications. These people don't deserve your time. Be around people who encourage you lift your mood and who respect you for who you are. As these people deserve your.

Time very much. Don't spend too much of your time with anyone you feel doesn't appreciate you completely. As these days go by you are developing a likeness and acceptance of yourself you are discovering what interests you. By adding these things to every day you live. When you like yourself as you are you will see how your world will change for the better. You will realize what you have to gain out of your life. Discover these strengths and use them more and more in Your life. Take care of yourself. Have pride and appreciate yourself just the way you are. Liking yourself is the first step to overcome any minor or major obstacle in your life. You have all of the resources within yourself to handle and overcome anything. You feel has been preventing you from getting. You to where you know in your heart where you really want to be. Life is about developing an appreciation and likeness of yourself. By doing what you enjoy doing the most. God is turning you into a positive accepting understanding endlessly loving kind hearted caring good.

Willed compassionate sympathetic empathetic person. You are doing well in your life because you have got God in your life. God is helping you by giving you God's wonderful amazing gifts talents superb magnificent rewards and blessings unto you. That God is blessing and rewarding you with each and every day you live. God will bless you and reward you with God's true loving riches for the rest of your life. Believe in The Lord your God always. God will always.

Be with you on Earth and in The Kingdom of Heaven For All of Eternity. God will decide when it is your time for you to be with God. In The Paradise of Heaven for all of Eternity. Don't fear death for after you die you will be born into Eternal Life in Heaven. With your Father God The Almighty. So believe in The Lord your God. For God has given you life and every person who is in your life. When you like yourself as you are. You will see your bad habits you use to have disappear into nothing. Make your own space in your own home. Your own space of rest and gathering of your thoughts. With your own Positive worthwhile good experiences. You have had and that are to come your way. You can organize yourself for bigger and greater opportunities and possibilities. That you can make for yourself to become part of your world. Everything that has happened to you in your life has meant to of happened. For you to be where you are at in your life now and these experiences have made you the person you are. God created you by giving you life on this Earth. God has.

Been with you through everything you have experienced in your entire lifetime past present future. God's love is everlasting on Earth and in the Kingdom of Heaven. God will continue to bless you with God's loving kind countless blessings. As you like the rest of us are very precious and valuable to God. God will always love you as God's love is eternal and everlasting. God will always bless you with lots of wonderful surprises each and every day you live. When you.

Do good in your life you will see how the good things that are happening to you are coming your way. We are all examples of each other. With how we live our lives by everything we do how we are as individuals. We are all learning from our own experiences. From every person we know from people we come across during our days. From people we are yet to meet in the future. By being at places like work at study at your activities of your interests. By being wherever we are meant to be at the right time and the right place. We are forever growing changing learning from our experiences. Giving out words of comfort joy and wisdom. By giving out these warm gestures of ourselves to people we are receiving All these things in return. When you respect yourself and like yourself as you are able to bring out the best in people you know. You can learn to look on the positive side of everything you go through. This will help you to work out your deepest concerns you then realize when you see the positive side of these hurdles that these things you thought were becoming an issue. For you weren't as concerning for you because you handled yourself with these issues in a positive way. The way.

To win friends and influence people in positive good healthy ways. Is by always being positive kind hearted good willed respectful considerate caring thoughtful supportive understanding compassionate sympathetic empathetic towards everyone. People will treat you the way you treat them as this is how we all learn from each other. You will gain more fulfillment when you are patient thoughtful.

Understanding and supportive to people you know and to people you come across. What you reap is what you sow. Always be there for those people you care for the most by continuing to be kind and supportive to them as this is what makes true solid genuine friendships that will last your lifetime. Every day we are experiencing Gods presence every day for the rest of our days on this Earth until our last day when we die our souls will be taken to the Kingdom of Kingdom of Heaven. Thank God for every day He is giving you and live forevermore you come across. Don't give anyone the power to destroy your own happiness. Look at those people in your life who are critical and insensitive you in a positive way. These people are giving you strength and determination In your life to get on and to succeed to the best of your potentials. If you can handle these difficult people then you can handle anyone. You can break the generational traits you see with your parents by working on changing your attitudes and behaviour towards yourself and to people you know and who you meet. Don't let these people make you unhappy instead work on making their affect have the reverse affect on you by being positive kind caring understanding forgiving patient accepting and giving always. We all have difficult.

Trials to get through from our past and present experiences. Time has a big part to play of our recoveries of the sufferings we have been through. Learn not to react to people when you feel them to be critical and insensitive towards you. Instead understand that we are all on our own different journeys in this life and we all handle our own sufferings. From our past and present experiences in different ways as we are all unique individuals. Forgive yourself and forgive.

Other people when you feel affected by them. Know that the reason why people can at times be critical and hurtful is because we are all suffering with our own issues in our lives. Don't give anyone the power to make you unhappy. Be aware that some people could try to say negative comments about you. You don't have to take any notice of these unnecessary comments because you know in your heart that these comments aren't true and you don't see yourself the way these people see you. The most important thing in life is how you see yourself if you like yourself just the way you are then what can go wrong in your world. Learn not to take on Board any negative comment from anyone as this is not your problem. Every day work on letting peoples negativity wash over you like water flows down a stream. In time you will get stronger with handling people who you feel are negative towards you. You will understand more and more. That they are the ones with the problem. You aren't the problem. Don't let their behaviour affect you in the slightest at all. Don't have contact with anyone who has any kind of negative affect on you. When you give out positivity love kindness.

Goodness respect consideration fairness justness. This is what you will receive in return. What you project out to people is what you will receive in return. What you worry about won't become true. Don't ever spend your time getting in a frenzied state. You will always be okay no matter what happens to you in your life. You can cope with anything and everything that happens to you. Believe this always know this even when you feel like things are getting on top of you.

As life is short why not put in a lot of effort into yourself everyday by learning from everything you go through and by working out ways of improving and bettering yourself until when you come to your last day of your life you will then look back and tell yourself I am so proud of myself for getting through every challenge I have had to go through in positive productive useful beneficial understanding calm and kind ways. Our beliefs within ourselves make us the people we are with all our learning experiences. By going through the tough times you have been through these times have helped you into the person you are by learning from everything you have Been through in your life. Be grateful for the pain you have had in your life as pain and suffering leads to positive and strong outcomes of all your efforts you have and are making now at this present moment. Every tough experience you go through something good and positive will come of it. Work towards becoming an optimistic person being this way will take you a long way in your life. Life is a journey of your spiritual growth. The things we do like our habits with what you watch on television the radio stations you listen to other.

Music that you like and that interests you what you eat and what you drink the work you do the interests you do the people you know and how you spend your time at home. Explains the person you are completely. Look for the good in people with their positive strengths when you do this you will see how people will take a shine to you by respecting you. We all want to feel important special appreciated understood and we want to feel like we are worth something to people.

How you treat everyone you come across is how you will be treated in return. Respect yourself and respect other people. You will gain complete satisfaction and joy by being kind to people. Try this you will be amazed at the results when you apply this in your life. Nobody can take away your own happiness. Have the determination not to let anyone do this. Be willing to listen to people and to offer your words of wisdom and comfort to those people you think could do with this. Don't let anyone affect your own peaceful state of joy and contentment you have the control to not let this happen. Work on rising above people like this when you do this you Will see how you will change for the better and you will notice how these people will change also by your influence. The most important thing in life is how you see yourself if you are happy with how you are then what does it matter about other people. Continue getting to know yourself very well by working hard on working through all of your issues in your life until you start to notice you are mastering this at comfortable and contented levels. When you start with this there will be nothing stopping you gaining the wonderful.

Benefits of your own success. What you fear doesn't become real. Learn to deal with your insecurities in productive ways by telling yourself everything will be okay no matter where you are as God is always with you wherever you are. God will always look after your needs for your whole stay on this Earth. When you believe in the Lord by confessing your sins and asking God to forgive you and always forgiving people when you feel hurt by them. For when you accept God in.

Your life you will see how God is always with you guiding and protecting you. How God is keeping you safe even when you might slightly feel unsafe. God will never let you down for God is completely faithful and sincere to those who love God. Coming from a dysfunctional family has its positive advantages. We all know that as children having difficult parents can lead to nervous breakdowns poor self esteem feeling unconfident about reaching out to other people and feeling worthless about yourself. On top of what can trigger off a nervous breakdown is if your parents get divorced. By going through these past experiences. You learn how you as An adult don't want to treat other people and you know in your heart that marriage is for life. You should be determined to do things differently than your parents did. Being aware of the mistakes your parents made and learning from them. By not allowing yourself to repeat these mistakes again. In other opportunities will help you to change your attitudes and behaviours in better ways in the right opportunities. Where God guides you to be. It is important not to rush into marriage. As you have got plenty of time to settle down with the right soul mate in the right time. God will direct your path

When both of you are completely ready. None of us know when our time is up this should encourage you to get on with it and fulfill your dreams. Why spend your time worrying about things. Worrying doesn't achieve anything it doesn't get you anywhere. Be optimistic always look on the bright side of all that happens to you. Be determined in your life to get where you really want to be. Accept people as they are know that what is meant to happen to you will happen to.

You like getting that perfect job doing what you have always wanted to do as an interest. Meeting that person you are meant to marry. Remember don't settle for second best ever. Work on strengthening your faith in God every day of your life. You have a lot to look forward to. To come in your future with lots of wonderful opportunities. Don't feel helpless about anything. Instead be grateful for all you have in your life. Be grateful for the place you live in. The wonderful people you know your health the fact you have got clothes to wear and food to eat. Be grateful that you have the ability And potential to communicate to walk to work to read to write to continually have good and stable friendships with your true friends. Who you have total respect and compassion for. Most importantly be grateful that you are alive on this Beautiful Earth. Remind yourself these things you have to be grateful for every day of your life. Always treasure and respect these people as you know how much these people mean to you. Work out what helps you to get through all of the issues you have from your past experiences and issues you have at this present moment that you feel are holding you back from progressing to comfortable levels of.

Your own well being of happiness. You have the potential and ability to work out all of your issues as you are the master of your life. You have all of the answers to everything you go through. This pain and suffering you have had in your life have been put there for good reasons. The most important reasons why you have had pain and suffering in your life is for you to develop your faith in the Lord Jesus Christ. This is the most and main important reason why you.

Have had pain and suffering in your life. Honour your Father in Heaven as God is your provider. God will always love you for all of Eternity. Move on from the people that hurt you the most. These people don't deserve your attention. These people aren't good for you. You are a completely different person with different qualities opinions and strengths. You have got your own life to live so live your life right away from these people. This will help you enormously in the long run. You will be so much happier and well balanced within Yourself in your life so start now and make the most important break You will ever make. Give out compassion understanding acceptance gratefulness consideration forgiveness and encouragement. When you do this you will see how you are helping your true friends in their own lives by helping them to see their own issues they are dealing with in their own lives in positive ways by your influence. The words that come out of your mouth with what you want to see happen in your life is what will happen to you in your.

Future always have a positive attitude with everything that happens to you. Realise and believe what is meant to happen to you will happen all in the right time. You can see the love of God from people who care about you. God's love is the strongest almightiest and everlasting love that will ever be. When you believe in The Lord Jesus Christ Almighty. You will see how God is blessing you in your life with the people you know. Who care for you so very much and you care so very much for these people. God has sent these people to you.

God works for good in miraculous ways. Believe in God and be thankful and grateful that God has thought of you by giving you the most precious and valuable thing that will ever be that is the gift of life. Believe in The Lord Jesus Christ Almighty. For when you do your life will change for the better. Every day pray for your needs with whatever you choose. Pray for those people you know who are in need. Your prayers are always heard by God. Don't let yourself fall down with despair. Instead look at the things you do have in your life that you are grateful and very glad for. Like those Precious and valuable people you know who really care about you. Who like you for how you are and who have stuck by you through the thick and the thin. This shows how much you care for these people and how much you like and enjoy their company and support. You know how much these special people mean to you so remember this in times of concern. These valuable people will always be there for you like you know you will always be there for them. You will.

Survive with everything that happens to you in your life. You can cope with. Everything and anything that happens to you because you have got your true friends that will stand by you always just like you will for them. Someone special will enter your life when you least expect it and when you are not looking for it. This is how it will happen for you. When you don't continually seek out to meet someone you will then have a much better aura about yourself and you will be amazed at how people will see you. They will see you in a.

Much more respecting and genuine way. Don't be in a hurry to meet anyone. Take your time by choosing your soul mate wisely and carefully as marriage is for life. Don't ever rush into any relationship with anyone. You have got plenty of time to get your relationship right always remember this. You will get there eventually. Use your time being single in productive constructive sensible enjoyable wonderful meaningful ways. Don't ever give up. Pray for God will always answer all of your prayers. In God's Perfect and Majestic Timing. God knows the right and best time when God will answer all of your prayers. Have faith love hope in God. God Adores you. Love your enemies. Show your respect consideration understanding acceptance compassion sympathy empathy genuine sincere honesty trustworthiness. To everyone you know and everyone you meet. Live your life without any regrets. Respect yourself and other people. Be grateful for every day you live. That God is giving you. Honour your Father God always. Without God you wouldn't be alive on this Earth. You are very special precious valuable important to God. You will always be loved by your Almighty Saviour God. From the beginning and until the end of your.

Time on this Earth. God knows you better than anyone. Get comfort and peace within yourself from the Lord Jesus Christ Almighty. For

God thought of you by giving you the most Precious and valuable gift you will ever receive that is life. Understanding the suffering and pain you have and are experiencing in your life has been put there for you to advance to mature to grow as a person to learn to accept yourself and other people. For you to believe in yourself for you to like the person you are despite how other people treat you. Build a very strong shield to protect yourself from.

Getting hurt. Know that in life it is okay to sometime give back to people in a slightly sarcastic way what they give to you. Remember to stand up for yourself when you feel you need to. We all have hurt and pain from our parents sisters brothers and from our partners at times in our lives. This is the process of life as we are all human and we are not perfect. Build your strength up to protect yourself from those people when you feel they are going out of their way to bring You down. When you feel they are trying to hurt you. Understand that the reason why your parents. Or whoever it is they are acting in this way is because they are unhappy in their own lives and when they see you positive and happy this is threatening them so they will try to bring you down to an unhappy level of emotion just like they feel within themselves. Understanding is the first step of dealing with your own hurt and pain appropriately calmly and wisely.

Learn not to take on board other peoples hurtful comments understand they are talking and expressing their own hurt and pain which they are trying to dump onto you. Rise above this negativity this is not at all good for you. God has designed life well. Amongst the hurt and pain we all experience from our parents sisters and brothers. There are lots of good things we can do to compensate from our hurts we feel our family put on us. Like you have the opportunity in your life. To fall in love with someone of the opposite sex. You can become very close to this person. Remember in any difficult environment wherever it is. God is with you always.

God knows exactly how you feel with everything you are going through in your life. Seek love and comfort in The Lord Jesus Christ Almighty. You will receive God's beautiful love in your life. Through your valuable friends and that special person. You know who cares for you through the thick and the thin. Don't ever lose hope in your life. Remind yourself of all these wonderful and amazing things that are happening to you in your life. Get rid of the negative things in your life by doing much more of the good things which bring you joy Fulfillment and happiness. Know that we all have wounds from our parents' sisters and brothers from our past and present experiences from our childhood. Adolescent years and our adult years. This is a completely natural process of our makeup of the person we are to this day. As we all have memories of all the experiences we have gone through. Of how we were and are being treated to this day. By our parents' sisters and brothers. Work on doing the things which provide you with comfort stability goodness helpfulness.

Gratefulness those good emotions come from your friendships your partner work and your interests. Always remember this. There will always be hope for you no matter what happens to you in your life.

Hold onto this thought. Practice easing and settling yourself amongst your inner emotional hurtful turmoil you experience every day. You will notice as you are getting older. Your tolerances to how you deal with your own inner self conflicts from the experiences you have been through with people. Has and is at this.

Present moment in time now in a lot better ways. Your own inner self strength is having the ability to deal with these unsettling emotions by getting the appropriate support from people who know you very well. These people have helped you to get through your difficulties and they have helped you to see your own struggles in helpful productive mature appropriate ways. Be very thankful appreciative grateful for these people as these people want to be of use and help to you like you want to be for them. Challenging tests have been put before you in your life for you to become. Emotionally stronger within yourself for you to use your determination at work and at your interests. For you to develop motivational skills so you can get on with what you really want to achieve in your life. Another positive thing you have developed and worked on in years is your true and solid friendships with those people you know you can count on through the good and the bad. Who you know are always there for you just like you are for them. Remember these positive things even in the hardest times. Know that in life.

You aren't always going to feel good and on top of things as this is the process and cycle of human nature. Find those things that will help you to get through your difficulties and that help you to cope with all you go through. When you discover these skills of coping even in the hardest of times you will see your own abilities and potentials of your own inner strength. When you get through any minor and or major difficulty yourself you will reap the rewards for you are the one that has got through these challenges with good support. Turn to The Lord by praying to Him about your.

Deepest concerns insecurities and worries for God will give you comfort and peace within yourself. From all your suffering you experience. You are never alone as God is always with you with all you go through. God will always be with you. Pray to your Father for whatever you wish to see happen in your life. God hears all of your prayers. God will answer all of your prayers in God's Perfect time. God has a wonderful plan for you in your life. Don't lose hope have faith for things to get better and improve. Know that your prayers Are always heard by God and these will be answered in God's Perfect time. You are made to cope with everything you go through. At times you will reach a point where you will feel like your issues are getting too much for you to handle. When you reach this point you will feel down and sad and even cry. This is completely natural. We all go through feeling this way as this is how we are built to feel down and sad about our circumstances in our lives. Life is a continual process of these cycles. Feeling good and content and then something happens that hurts you and you then feel sad and down.

These are normal and natural emotions that we all go through. This is the cycle of life that we as humans go through every day. Help yourself by reaching out by getting the appropriate support from your friends and from a counsellor as this will help you so much in the long run. We all need each other and we all need support. You are going to be okay with all you have to face and deal with in your life. Hold on to your faith in God. Get to really know what helps you to cope in your life. By dealing with difficult people.

Holding down your job maintaining your home spending your money wisely being around people who know you feel are good for your well being. By doing an interest which you know you will enjoy. You know those people you can truly count on through the good and the bad. Turn to these people when you feel you need to. Use your own coping resources to help you to carry on in your life. You are in charge of making all of your decisions. You have the choice with how you react to every person you know and to people You come In contact with throughout your days. Life is about fulfilling your dreams by making your dreams come true. Work on yourself by working through all your issues with the right support. You will see when you work through your issues small and large how much better you will feel within yourself. You will have a sense of proudness about yourself of getting through things because you have chosen to handle your issues appropriately. By reaching out to those people who you know can give you the right support and best advice.

There is support for you which you can seek no matter what you are going through in your life. Do those things that bring you pleasure and happiness like working seeing your good friends having parties going out to interesting places with your friends. Continue pursuing your interests regularly. Also hold on to your hope that you will meet someone who will meet your needs completely and who will cherish you for the rest of your life. Don't be hard on yourself for the things you don't have in your life. Instead look at your wonderful.

Progress you have and are making in your life with all the things you have and are doing now. Work is not only going to a job and getting paid for all your efforts. Work can come from working through your issues in your life having friendships by supporting and serving friends writing about your life experiences. By doing this is helping yourself and your friends and keeping your place clean and tidy for yourself and your guests conveniences and satisfactions. All of these things are forms of work which you are doing for yourself and for people you know who really appreciate all of Your own unique and valuable efforts. Don't lose hope with finding a suitable job for yourself and don't lose hope with meeting someone special and genuine. Both of these things will come your way when they are meant to in the right time. Make the most of your free time in productive ways. Like keep up looking in the papers for work and organizing interviews week after week. Also send your resume with a cover letter to lots and lots of different companies. The more you do this the more practice and experience you are gaining and you are becoming more and more motivated and.

Determined by doing this as a result. Apply for as many jobs in reception office assistant retail and to work in a café as much as you possibly can. Continue being determined motivated and wise in your consistency of all your efforts in applying for jobs. Remember to rise above the knockbacks. You are a winner. Continue on your journey in this wonderful yet at times disappointing adventure that is life. God is always keeping you safe by protecting you from evil every waking and sleeping moment you live each and every day.

God will always keep you safe. God loves you very much so believe in your Father Almighty. God has lots of wonderful surprises in store to come for you in your future. Look after your own health as this is very important for yourself in your future. God blesses those people who believe in Him and who do good to themselves and other people. God also blesses those who want to help and improve themselves. As being this way is good for yourself and is also very helpful and beneficial for people who you know and to people you Meet. Your influence with all the things you do in your life encourages and helps people you know extremely well. Just like how this works the other way also with other people you know who You feel are good role models for you. Make the time you spend on your own special comfortable and interesting. Every day when you have the time to yourself use your time productively efficiently and easily in relaxing ways. You are the master of your life. You choose how you wish to live your life by doing whatever you want to do in your life. You choose your friends you choose your career you choose what you eat you choose how you feel you.

Choose where you want to live and you choose your partner. All of these things have. Come from your own judgement from your own liking and you have made all of these decisions yourself. Remind yourself every day of your own wonderful progress you have and are making. You are the one that deserves credit because you are the one each and every time who is bringing yourself up through every difficulty you experience. Just importantly your friends are the ones who have helped you to be the strong motivated.

And determined person you are and who you know you will always be for the rest of your life. Listen to yourself with everything you experience. We are all on our own unique paths in our lives. You know yourself better than anyone knows you. Always remember this even in the most difficult of times. You know how to pick up yourself back up again even in the most despairing of times. Don't take any notice of other people's immature behaviour you see happening Around you. Choose your friends carefully and wisely. You know what you really want to achieve in your life. You know what steps to take in achieving all of your goals small and large. Start now by making those important steps of working on being where you really want to be in your life. There is no better time than right now. Make the changes you feel are vital for your own well being. Your own well being and your own state of happiness. When you start making these changes there will be nothing stopping you. We are forever changing growing maturing learning gaining knowledge.

And wisdom. Go for it. Don't let any positive opportunity pass you by. Take every positive opportunity you can as life is short. Every day work hard on changing what is concerning you the most in your life.

You have all of the resources and the intelligence to know how you are going to go about changing your habits. No matter how short or long you have had this problem. Start now by making all of the steps you know of that will put you on the right path. You can succeed.

On this new exciting and wonderful journey that will open so many doors for you in your life. Understand that some of us move on from our families. You are either lucky and you come from a good stable family or you are less fortunate and you come from a dysfunctional family. If you come from a dysfunctional family it is not the end of the world. You can make your own life just as good for yourself. By having supportive and understanding friends that you know will always be there for you no matter what you go through. Working in a field of your choice that you know you will excel In and doing interests of your choice that you know you are good at that you know you will enjoy thoroughly. Work hard on making these things become a part of your life. You like the rest of us deserve to have these positive things in your life. Don't waste any of your time. Start now by entering your new and exciting journey of your life. Don't waste any of your time. Start now by entering your new and exciting journey of your life. There will be no going back when you start on this wonderful journey you have created yourself. Be proud of all.

Your achievements small and large. You are going to make it without a doubt. In this world it is important to feel comfortable being the person you are. To like yourself as you are. If you don't like yourself as you are you will find it difficult to progress and move on in your life. Make your own time you have enjoyable productive relaxing. The time you have on your own is very precious valuable energizing for your existence and for your progress to get on. Always rely on yourself with everything you experience as you know.

What is best for you in your life. You don't have to do anything you don't want to do. You don't have to be friends with anyone you don't want to be friends with. Be selective of who you are friends with. As some people aren't good for you. God can help you with anything that is concerning you the most in your life. Pray to God and ask God to help you with what is concerning you the most. Your Father in Heaven hears all of your prayers. God wants to help you because God loves you very much. You are very special precious valuable to God. God is with you always. God will always be with you For your whole entire stay on this Earth. Believe in The Lord Jesus Christ when you do you will see how God will transform you into a beautiful giving person. Honour your Father always and all will go well for you. Don't assume the worst with people's comments. Understand that the way people speak to you is the way they know how from their own experiences from their own past and present in their lives. You only know how you feel with all of the experiences you have been.

Through in your life. You don't know how other people feel within themselves. You don't know what other people have to deal with in their own lives. Don't always be sensitive with what people talk to you about. Instead understand that these people are struggling with their own major issues in their own lives. Accepting and understanding where other people are coming from is the first step of dealing with your own maturity and your own attitudes towards how you deal with all types of people. This is the first step of improving and handling yourself in more appropriate mature and wiser.

Ways in your own life. The most important thing in life is how you see and feel within yourself. By doing what makes you feel good and happy. A very important lesson in life is not to let what people say to you bring you down even if you feel this is their intention. Don't put yourself through any form of misery just because you feel someone is trying to get to you. Instead distance yourself from this person and learn to stand up for yourself with this person when you feel you need to. You don't have to let this person affect you. Don't give this person the power to destroy your own happiness it really Isn't worth it for your own sake. Work on yourself by achieving your goals with your friendships finding a job continuing going to your interest and looking after yourself completely. All of these things are very important for your own well being and happiness. Don't have as much contact with people you feel aren't good for your growth as you are your own person. Be careful with how much you give of yourself to people who you feel take advantage of you.

Who you feel don't respect your own unique opinions of how you see certain views of life. Not everyone will give back to you respectfully and equally how much you give out to them. You need to protect yourself by not being as available to these people. You will be the one who will be let down and walked over. So spend your time working towards what you really want to see happen in your life. Be around those people who you feel give back to you respectfully and equally. These people are good for you. For your growth.

Understanding acceptance confidence maturity and your own individuality. Understand as none of us are perfect and we are all different from time to time you will disagree with people's opinions and advice. This won't happen all the time but it will happen from time to time. At times when you both disagree with your opinions you will experience uncomfortable emotions. Because both of you are experiencing tension from not agreeing on a very comfortable level. This can cause you to feel down upset and frustrated. Realizing that what works for one person with coping with your own issues isn't going to have the same Effect with another person. As we are all different and we all cope differently with our own experiences. What might feel hard for you to handle in your life might not be hard for another person to handle. We are all on our own unique and individual paths in our lives with different expectations different goals different coping strategies and different strengths. When you realize this this will help you to know the only person you can rely on is yourself so really like yourself as you are because if you don't who will. You are not always going to be able to please everyone. Be aware that.

People will try to bring you down when they see you doing well in your life. This happens because none of can always be happy and on top of things. You will at times have to face people when they are having hard moments in their lives. This isn't easy to deal with for any of us and you will be affected in negative ways as a result. This can lead to feelings of sadness despair and feelings of hopelessness. This happens to all of us. We all get hurt from people in life. It is important to learn to like yourself as you are and to develop.

Numerous coping strategies for yourself to cope in these situations. Life wasn't meant to be easy for any of us. We all have pain of some sort or another to cope with. Find out what helps to ease the pain you experience in your life. Be open to discovering these helpful outlets for yourself as these outlets for yourself as these outlets are vital for your own survival. The only way that we are going to learn the important lessons that we need to learn is through pain. It is like this for every single person on this Earth. You are not the Only person who experiences hardships we all do. Find those things that will ease the pain you experience in your life. Find those things that bring you peace comfort and joy. You will find every time when you get through any difficulty in your life you will discover. You will learn the important lessons you are meant to learn. Don't be hard on yourself through these times. Instead let yourself feel frustrated until you reach a level of letting yourself realize and learn what you feel you need to learn from these experiences.

Know that in life people won't always meet your needs how you would like them to. Your Father God has complete unconditional love care interest support inspiration and gratefulness for you. We are walking and talking images of God. We are following the footsteps of Christ in our daily lives. God is guiding you every moment and in every footstep you take. We all have the Holy Spirit within us with God's presence and God's will. Believe in your Father in Heaven for when you do you will see how God is changing you and you will see how God is working in miraculous ways in your life.

Share your glory with others as this is good for your growth and people will look up to you in their own way. When you are doing well in your own life you will notice people's strengths within themselves rather than their weaknesses. How you see yourself in your life with your hopes and your dreams you want to make happen for yourself is turning you into the person you know in your heart you really want to be and who you are meant to be. Make the journey you are on in your life full of interesting adventurous enjoyable fun and Positive experiences that you will never forget. You are just as important as the next person and you have a purpose and meaningful reasons why you are here on this Earth. When you do you will see the doors of goodness joy and glory open before your very eyes. The more you like yourself for who you are. The more you work on yourself by doing the things to improve yourself the better you will see that you will become. Have faith in The Lord Jesus Christ Almighty. God can bring you out of any dark place you have been in through into God's shining light. God wants to give you God's love.

Through your true friends through your work through your interests and through your partner. God will always protect you bless you and look after you for your whole stay on this Earth until God decides it is time for you to join God in The Kingdom of Heaven. God will always love you on Earth and in Heaven so believe in The Lord Jesus Christ Almighty. For all good comes from your Father. Don't be afraid of anything as God is always with you. Listen to yourself always with.

Everything you have to deal with and with what you are planning to achieve in your life. Continue asserting yourself as much as you feel you need to with those people you feel treat you unfairly. These people need to hear you make your stances. This is good for your own importance existence and for your own happiness and survival in your own life. For your own sake and your own only. Don't be around people who you feel criticize you who you feel don't accept you for how you are. These people aren't good for you. These people are getting and gaining pleasure from themselves when they Bring you down by saying hurtful comments to you. You don't have to be like these people. One way to handle these people is to show your kindness to them when you feel they are hurting you as this will be like coals of fire burning on their heads. Remember this always. Create a new beginning for yourself in your life. By placing everything in this new beginning to be good healthy positive. You are a new person with positive expectations maturity wisdom. As you are getting older you are changing and you are developing more mature appropriate wiser coping skills. You are also.

Developing a positive and wiser outlook of yourself and other people's understanding with their needs. By putting yourself in these people's shoes. By doing this you can feel and experience in your own way what these people are going through in their own lives. This is a very important skill to have and to always have. As having this skill will take you along way in your life. You will notice that people will respect you and look up to you when you show your compassion understanding patience thoughtfulness and when you are.

Just yourself. As we are all on our own unique paths in our lives. We have all come from different backgrounds with how we felt we were treated as children and adolescence. You have now entered and formed your new beginning as a responsible efficient capable well preserved mature wise individual. The road you are now on will only get better and you will continue to get stronger more mature more capable and more experienced by developing more and more resourceful tools. You will always have and remember for You to cope in any and every situation you will be in for the rest of your life. We are all teachers of our own experiences. We all have our own unique important valuable and special example which we are forever helping sharing guiding learning from and setting for ourselves and other people the examples we are destined to. When you can see people's strengths gifts and positive qualities you will be amazed at the results of your time well shared. With your patience consideration towards these people and the fact that you are being selfless. By offering your full self to these very special.

And valuable people who you know means so much to you Your true friends are really the ones you owe all of your goodness and truth to. As these people are the ones who have brought you through from all the experiences you have been through into the person you have become to this day. You know your friends would do anything for you and you know you would do anything for them. Your friends have even helped you to get the confidence to take on even bigger and greater goals with their everlasting kind and caring.

Support your friends have also helped you to develop as a person to mature and to gain with wisdom. All of this has now helped you to form a new exciting and special relationship with that person you are meant to meet and to share your experiences with. Things in your life will only get better. Get rid of what you know in your heart you don't want in your life anymore. Fill your thoughts for your well being. In healthy loving caring kind ideals which you know will be purifying and will always be good for yourself in your Life what you don't want to be a part of your life has now gone and all the positive things you really want to be a part of your life will remain. These things are making you feel good satisfied and happy every day you live by Gods grace. Things are looking up for you on this new road you agree on. There will never be any going back. You are going to continue to bloom and grow stronger with your friendships your work your interests your faith in God. With that special person.

Who you are meant to be with. As God has been the One that has changed you into this person. By the power of the Holy Spirit. Your Father in Heaven because God loves you. When you are interacting with people work on responding to these people in positive mature appropriate kind ways. When you present yourself with these qualities you will see how much people will admire and respect you for having these qualities. Being this way will help you to understand people more and by really feeling like what another person is experiencing in their life. Show your compassion and

Consideration to people. When you do you will see how this will come back to you. What you give out you will get back in return. Look at all the people in your life which you are helping supporting your attention to and guiding you on the right path. You mean so much to these people like they mean to you. Work on achieving your own goals by working so you have more joy to bring to your friendships with these people and for yourself as well. Working on having productive structure in your week and work on what will help you hold down your job successfully in stable ways. God works Wonders with you God can mend your health lead you on the right path to meet those very precious and valuable people you are meant to know. God brings people of the opposite sex together who with God's grace are meant to be with one another to share special experiences that will be remembered. Believe in the Lord for when your heart is open to God you will see how God is blessing you abundantly each and every day you live. You are entering a new awakening by God's grace through the Holy Spirit. God has the power of goodness to bring you out from the dark place you were in.

Through into the new bright and positive place where you are now meant to be and where you will always remain as for when positive changes will continue to happen. Use your time how you choose to.

By doing the things that make you happy. These things can be from your friendships from your interests that you are gifted in and where your strengths lye the most and by working in a field that you know you are good at. These are all forms in different ways of work.

Work doesn't only come from going to a job and getting paid to work. You are working by supporting and serving your friends by sharing your words of wisdom through your thoughts with guidance from the Holy Spirit by God. Be happy with where you are at in your life and work on what you feel you need to improve. Realize that it isn't good to give too much of yourself to everyone. Especially to those people you feel who betray your good morals and who you feel don't respect your good progress you have and are making in your life. Don't give so much of yourself to those People who you feel take advantage of your goodness as these people aren't good for you. They will only hurt you for with some people this is their aim to set you back stay away from these people. When your outlook changes about yourself and about people around you as you get older. You will be amazed with the things you discover yourself doing. You can do these positive things in your life because your outlook has changed. You have become an optimistic person with zest positive with positive strengths potentials abilities.

You have probably noticed that people are attracted to you as a person because of your positive attitudes towards yourself with how you hold yourself in your life and with how you treat people you know and who you meet. You will never lose these positive qualities as these great qualities have become the person you are. They are a part of you they come from your heart. You have been training yourself by learning from others exactly each and every positive qualities you have. You will continue to gain and learn more and more knowledge of learning from what you do. From other people by developing more and even greater positive qualities.

As you continue growing every day on your journey in your life. God is blessing you with God's love each day you live. Give your thanks to the Lord Jesus Christ as God has given you the gift of life. God made you God thought to give you the gift of life. For God created you in God's Image. You can see God's love shining through from people's kind caring understanding support they are continually giving to you. You Are doing the same in return. You care for these people just

As much as they care for you. This is how God made you and all of us. Your Father in Heaven is a very loving forgiving caring understanding helpful powerful amazing and forever giving of God's love to everyone of God's children throughout all ends of this Earth. God will always open God's loving hands by blessing you abundantly every day for the rest of your life. Your inner beauty of goodness shines through your words of comfort joy wisdom. Through your natural and flowing body rhythm in your life. When you come in contact.

With all kinds of people who are all on different paths in their lives. That God has chosen for you also. When you feel good about being the person you are you will notice how people notice this about you.

They will admire you for this. Continue making outstanding and positive progress in your life. For God sees all your good works to yourself and other people with your intentions. As your Father in Heaven knows you even better than you know yourself. God is the Almightiest.

Creator that will ever be to remain in Heaven for Eternity. You have the chance to be with your Father in Heaven if you believe in God. You have transformed into the person you are by learning from yourself and other peoples attitudes that will always be with you for the rest of your life. You have got so much more to learn in your life by being in many more situations. At work at your interests different places with your friends and with your soul mate sharing both of your experiences closely. Work on strengthening your faith in the Lord by going to church sharing your beliefs of how you feel about what God is doing for you in your life. Also talk to Other Christians about their beliefs and their faith in God. This is a great way to talk to other Christians about their beliefs and their faith in God. There is so much to learn in life. Be open and interested in learning more about life. Discover the reasons why you think you are here on this Earth. Get in touch with what you really think is your mission and purpose on this Earth. Ask God to reveal these answers to you. We all need to feel like we are achieving positive things in our lives.

By doing this you gain confidence self worth and you feel important. Like you are worth something in this world. It is important to work to have an interest to go to have supportive and understanding friends.

Who you know will always be there for you no matter what. It is important to fall in love with someone you feel is compatible to you and for this person to feel like you are compatible for them. We are all made to meet that special person to share our experiences with. You will in the right time meet that special.

Person who will make you very happy who will meet your needs completely. Move on from those people you feel don't appreciate you completely. These people aren't good for you. They will just drag you down. Some people do this when they see you are doing well in your life. They can try to do and say hurtful things and words because they are jealous of your positive qualities that they don't have. Don't let these kinds of people get to you. These people aren't worth your worry. Be with people you feel respect you completely. Who you feel you can be yourself around. In completely relaxed and contented ways. Realize that you aren't going to get the Complete respect and positive encouragement from everyone. You will receive total respect and positive support from those genuine people you know who you can count on through the thick and the thin. As life is short why not do and be what you have always dreamed of doing. Don't waste any of your time. Continue organizing as many interviews as possible until you find the most suitable job that you know you will be able to manage and you know you will like. Think of the life skills you have and use this knowledge into working in a field where your strengths lye the most. Along with your gifts and talents. You have all that it takes to work in a suitable field of work where you will be employed for a long time. Keep on searching for this suitable job until you find it. When this job comes your way when it is meant to. You will find yourself growing to like and enjoy your work. You will also see how you will excel by doing the tasks that you know you are able to do. When you are meeting someone of the opposite sex for the first time don't get your hopes up to high. Also don't expect this person to be the person of your dreams. As not every person who you feel likes you will meet your standards and morals. Always get to know any person you feel you would like to get to know as a friend first. Never rush into anything with this person. Be choosy and very selective with who you get to know. As your own safety and your own happiness is most important always. Never settle for second best as this only leads to insecurity and unhappiness. You deserve the very best in your life with lots of good positive and worthwhile opportunities which will come your way. If you take all the Right steps for the opening of a wonderful life that you deserve completely. Be patient. As good things come to those who wait. God wants you and all God's children to be wise sensible selective with who you chose to turn to about your own personal business and successes. God wants you to have a long happy healthy prosperous life. Learn not to be trusting too soon of people you meet for the first time as not every one can be trusted. Make it your main focus in your life to be wise careful and sensible with everything you do always. Learn from your own and other people's mistakes. Don't be too open and friendly with every person you meet as not everyone is trustworthy and honest. Remember you don't have to be friends with anyone you don't want to be friends with and you are under no obligation to tell anyone who you don't want to tell anything about yourself that you don't wish to share. Be careful of some people because there are people out there who have jealousy in their hearts of yours and other people's successes. You can't trust everyone. Stay away from these people these people aren't at all good for your well being and happiness. Have more to do with those people who are positive encouraging joyful to be around supportive who you know have your best interests in their hearts for you and who you can genuinely trust completely.

www.ingramcontent.com/pod-product-compliance
Lightning Source LLC
Chambersburg PA
CBHW020346130626
46549CB00003B/1327